Super-Duper Science

Wacky Weather!

by Annalisa McMorrow

illustrated by Marilynn G. Barr

  To Kimmie

Publisher: Roberta Suid
Design & Production: Scott McMorrow
Cover Design: David Hale
Cover Art: Mike Artell
Copy Editor: Carol Whiteley

Also by the author: *Save the Animals!* (MM1964), *Love the Earth!* (MM1965), *Learn to Recycle!* (MM1966), *Sing a Song About Animals* (MM1987), *Preschool Connections* (MM1993), *Incredible Insects! (and Spiders, Too)* (MM2018), *Spectacular Space!* (MM2019), *Outstanding Oceans!* (MM2020), *Ladybug, Ladybug* (MM2015), *Twinkle, Twinkle* (MM2016), *Rub-a-Dub-Dub* (MM2017), *Daffy-Down-Dilly* (MM2037), *Pussycat, Pussycat* (MM2036), *Rain, Rain, Go Away!* (MM2038), *Amazing Animals!* (MM2059), and *Peculiar Plants!* (MM2058).

For a complete catalog, please write to the address below:
P.O. Box 1680
Palo Alto, CA 94302 U.S.A.

Call us at: 1-800-255-6049
E-mail us at: MMBooks@aol.com

Visit our Web site:
http://www.mondaymorningbooks.com

Monday Morning Books is a registered trademark of
Monday Morning Books, Inc.

ISBN 1-57612-043-0

Printed in the United States of America
987654321

Contents

Introduction 4
All About Weather 6

Hands-On Discoveries
Moonbow Mural 8
Colors of Rain and Snow 10
Raining Fish and Lizards 11
Making Mirages 14
Hailstone Weigh-In 16
Glow-in-the-Dark Clouds 17
Funny Forecasts 19
Jack Frost Fun 21
Terrible Tornado Game 22
Super-Duper Project:
    Weather Watchers 26

Nonfiction Book Links
Weather Glossaries 28
Seasonal Spelling 31
Interview a Cloud 35
Lightning Reports 38
Animal Weather Report 40
Amazing Auroras 43
Super-Duper Project:
    Interplanetary Weather 44

Fiction Book Links
The Wizard of Oz 48
The Blizzard of Oz 49
The Story of a Boy... 50
Rhymes with "Snow" 51
The Stranger 52
Summer All the Time 53
Water Dance 54
I Am... 55
The Snow Queen 56
The Sun Queen 57
Super-Duper Project:
    Writing a Retold Tale 58

It's Show Time!
Wacky Weather Program 60
"Snow Business..." 61
Snow Costume 62
"Lightning Bolts" 63
Thundercloud Costume 64
"Let's Go to the Equator" 65
"Hurricane" 65
"Tornados Start Out..." 66
"Rainbows and Moonbows" 67
Rainbow Costume 68

Resources
Super-Duper Fact Cards 69
Weather A to Z List 77
Beaufort Wind Scale/El Niño 78
Nonfiction Resources 79
Web Site Addresses 80

Introduction: Why Weather?

Weather can be giant (hailstones larger than grapefruits have fallen), combustible (lightning can set things on fire), colorful (algae can turn snow green), bizarre (rain during a moonlit night can cause a moonbow), and all-around wacky!

Children will learn about the exciting weather world while practicing writing, reading, researching, performance, and speaking skills. They'll learn about the six types of lightning, interview clouds, weigh a hailstone, explore waterspouts, star in a musical review, and much more. Most of the activities can easily be simplified for younger children or extended for upper grades. This book will enhance learning in many subjects through exploration of the weather in our world.

Wacky Weather! is divided into four parts (plus a resource section). **Hands-On Discoveries** contains activities that allow children to participate in answering science questions they may have, for example, "What are mirages?" or "How are rainbows made?" Reproducible sheets have directions or information written specifically for the children. These sheets are marked with a special cloud icon.

Nonfiction Book Links features speaking, writing, and reporting activities based on nonfiction resources. Most activities are accompanied by helpful handouts that lead children through the research procedure. When research is required, you have the option of letting children look for the facts needed in the library (or in books you've checked out ahead of time). Or they may use the "Super-Duper Fact Cards" located in the resource section at the back of this book. These cards list information for 16 types of weather. Duplicate the cards onto neon-colored paper, and cut them out. Laminate them, and cut them out again, making sure to leave a thin laminate border to prevent peeling. Keep the cards in a box for children to choose from when doing their research. These cards also provide an opportunity for younger children to do research by giving them needed information in a simple, easy-to-understand format.

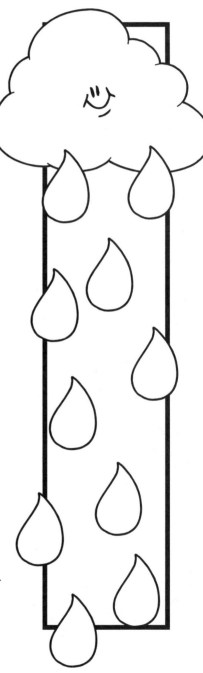

The Fiction Book Links section uses storybooks and chapter books to introduce information about interesting types of weather, such as the tornado in *The Wizard of Oz*. This section's activities, projects, and language extensions help children connect with weather. Each "Link" also includes a tongue twister. You can challenge children to create their own twisters from the weather facts they've learned. Also included in this section are decorating suggestions for "setting the stage" for each particular book.

It's Show Time! presents new songs sung to old tunes, and costume suggestions for putting on a performance. The songs can be duplicated and given to the children. If you want to hold a performance, write each performer's name on the reproducible program page and give copies to your audience.

Each of the first three sections ends with a "Super-Duper Project," an activity that uses the information children have learned in the unit. These projects include tracking weather forecasts, giving a weather report, and writing and retelling a famous tale. A choral performance is a possible "Super-Duper" ending for the "It's Show Time!" section.

At the end of the book are nonfiction resources to share with children, such as information about El Niño. Also included are weather-related Web sites to explore.

Suggestions for Extending Lessons:
• Have the children watch the weather report on TV.
• Bring in newspaper weather reports for children to read. Chart the reports to see how often the newspapers are correct.
• Have children observe the weather each day and chart it on a calendar.
• Invite a meteorologist to talk to the students.

All About Weather

What Is Weather?

When we talk about the weather, we want to know whether it is warm and sunny outside, or cold, or snowing, or raining. Weather describes what is happening outside.

Earth is covered by a layer of gasses held in place by gravity. This is the atmosphere. We live in the atmosphere, the enormous ocean of air that surrounds Earth. Weather refers to the state of the atmosphere at any given time or place.

How Does Weather Change?

Air masses cover our entire planet. Each air mass has layers of air that are about the same temperature and moisture throughout. The temperature and moisture in an air mass depend on where the air mass formed. If it formed over a desert, an air mass would tend to be hot and dry. If it formed over a tropical ocean, an air mass might be hot and wet.

Air masses continually move, changing temperature and shape. They move because the Earth rotates and because of the sun. The sun heats Earth more at the equator than at the poles. Warmed air rises and cooled air sinks, so at the equator the air rises and flows toward the poles. At the polar regions, the cooled air sinks and moves toward the equator.

While this north-south air movement goes on, the Earth rotates eastward. This combination causes air masses to move.

A front is where the edges of two air masses of different temperatures meet. Most weather changes take place as a front passes by. A cold front could bring a cooler summer day, or a freezing winter day.

Predicting the Weather

Meteorologists are people who forecast the weather. They make their reports based on information from weather instruments and satellites. They predict how the weather will change based on records of past weather patterns and their understanding of nature. But no one can guess exactly how the weather will be.

Weather Map

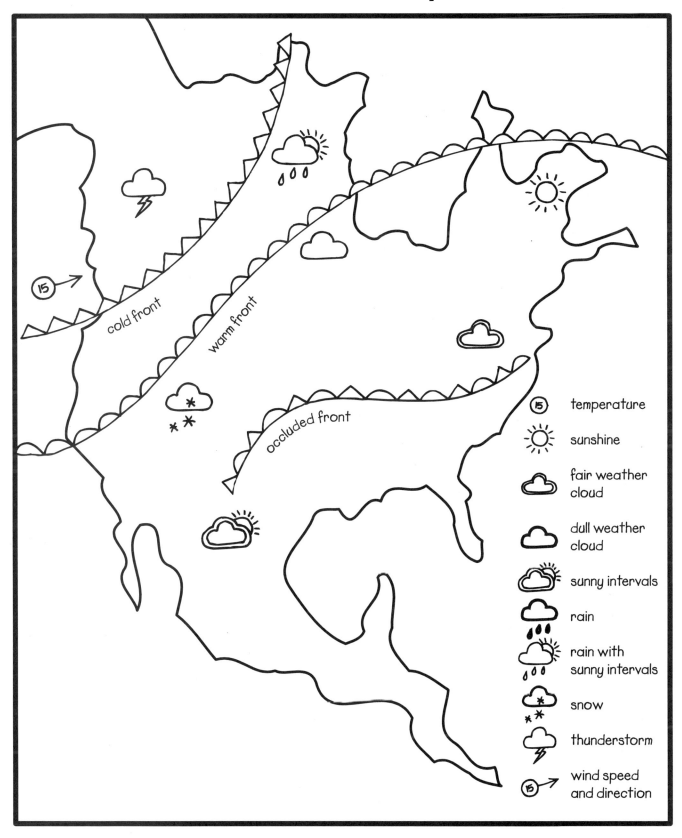

cold front

warm front

occluded front

15 →

15   temperature

☼   sunshine

fair weather cloud

dull weather cloud

sunny intervals

rain

rain with sunny intervals

snow

thunderstorm

wind speed and direction

Moonbow Mural

For a rainbow to be formed, there must be water droplets in the air and there must be light. Moonbows can be found after it rains on the night of a full moon, just after the moon has risen.

Materials:
"Making a Rainbow" Hands-on Handout (p. 9), small mirrors, shallow pans of water, pencils, crayons (in rainbow colors), black construction paper, colored chalk (in rainbow colors), tape

Directions:
1. Divide children into teams and give each team a copy of the "Making a Rainbow" Hands-on Handout.
2. Have the teams work together to make rainbows. Make sure children observe the colors of the rainbows.
3. Remind the children of the order of the colors in a rainbow or moonbow: red, orange, yellow, green, blue, indigo, and violet. Teach them a mnemonic to remember the order, for example, Roy G. Biv. Or let them make up their own mnemonics.
4. Tape sheets of black construction paper together to make a large, mural-sized canvas.
5. Have children work together to color a moonbow on the paper.
6. Post the finished moonbow on one wall of the classroom.

Note:
For more information about rainbows, refer to the "Super-Duper Fact Card" (p. 73).

Fun Fact:
In Queensland, Australia, the Kabi worship a god who is half fish and half snake. Called Dhakhan, the god appears as a rainbow in the sky as he moves from the holes in which he lives.

Making a Rainbow

Materials:
Pocket mirror, shallow pan of water, pencil, crayons (red, orange, yellow, green, blue, indigo, purple)

Directions:
1. Put the pan of water in a sunlit place opposite a white wall.
2. Hold the mirror at one end of the pan so that the sunlight strikes it.
3. Move the mirror until you see the colors of the rainbow on the wall. Then answer the questions below.

Questions:
1. How many colors can you see in the rainbow?

_____

_____

2. Name the colors.

_____

_____

3. Draw a picture of the rainbow below.

Wacky Weather! ©1998 Monday Morning Books, Inc.

Colors of Rain and Snow

Small bits of reddish soil in the air colored rain (and snow) in Italy in 1755. In 1933, black rain fell in New York State and brown rain fell in Vermont after a dust storm filled the air with swirling dust. Green rain fell on Moscow in 1987, most likely colored by green pollen in the air.

Materials:
Drawing paper, crayons or markers, watercolors, straws

Directions:
1. Share the above facts with the children.
2. Give each child a piece of drawing paper and a variety of crayons. Have children draw pictures of people or landscapes.
3. Provide a variety of watercolors for children to drip onto their pictures. They can choose colors that match the different colors it has rained (as listed above). Children can use straws to blow the drips of paint to make rain-streaked pictures.
4. Once the pictures are dry, post them on a bulletin board.

Options:
• Cut raindrop shapes from thick paper and let children paint these. Use clothespins to hang the raindrops from a clothesline stretched across the classroom.
• Let children make colored snow pictures using colored cotton balls. There have been recorded instances of pink snow and green snow in the western United States and in Canada.

Fun Fact:
Red and silver maples and poplar trees turn up their leaves when rain threatens.

Raining Fish and Lizards

Waterspouts are like tornados, but they form over seas, lakes, or rivers. (Or they are tornados that move over water and suck water up into their whirling winds.) The winds in a waterspout move more slowly than the winds in a regular tornado. The swirling tubes of water can suck up fish as they whirl. Sometimes they drop the fish several miles (km.) away. Waterspouts are responsible for unusual "rains."

Materials:
"What's in a Waterspout?" Hands-on Handout (p. 12), "Fish and Friends Patterns" (p. 13), globe, rulers, pencils, crayons or markers, scissors, glue, gray construction paper

Directions:
1. Give each child a copy of the "What's in a Waterspout?" Hands-on Handout and a copy of the "Fish and Friends Patterns."
2. Have the children cut out the patterns and color them as desired.
3. Let children make waterspouts from gray construction paper. They can make the waterspouts look funnel-like. Show them pictures in a book, or the one in the margin.
4. Children can glue the animals to the waterspouts.
5. Post the finished waterspouts on a "Wacky Waterspouts" bulletin board. Post a copy of the "What's in a Waterspout?" Hands-on Handout nearby.

Fun Fact:
The highest waterspout occured in 1898 in Australia. It was 5,015 ft. (1,528 m.) high and 10 ft. (3.1 m.) across.

What's in A Waterspout?

On October 23, 1947, fish (some as long as a pencil) rained down on the town of Marsville, Louisiana. Measure your pencil and write the length down here. Then write down what you would do if it rained fish on your town!

_____

_____

_____

_____

Live lizards rained down on Montreal in 1857. Find Montreal on the globe. Which do you think would be worse to have rain on you: fish or snails? Why?

_____

_____

_____

_____

_____

In 1881, in Worcester, England, it rained crabs and periwinkles (a type of snail). Find England on the globe.

Wacky Weather! © 1998 Monday Morning Books, Inc.

Fish and Friends Patterns

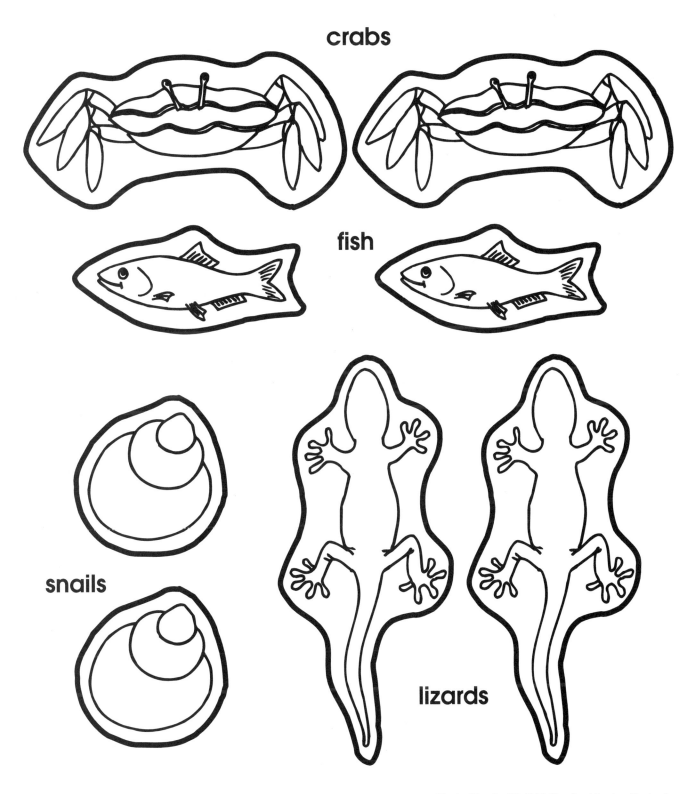

crabs

fish

snails

lizards

Wacky Weather! © 1998 Monday Morning Books, Inc.

Making Mirages

Mirages are optical illusions. They can often be seen over hot roads or deserts. Mirages occur where a layer of cold air lies over a layer of light, warm air. The light is bent as it passes through air of different densities. This can make a piece of the sky appear on the ground, looking like a blue puddle of water.

Materials:
"Now You See It" Hands-on Handout (p. 15), clear cellophane, colored construction paper, paste, scissors, markers, tape

Directions:
1. Give each child a copy of the "Now You See It" Hands-on Handout to observe.
2. Explain that children will be making their own mirages.
3. Provide colored construction paper for children to use to draw pictures of deserts.
4. Give each child a sheet of clear cellophane. Have children cut out desert oasis designs from the colored construction paper and paste these on the clear cellophane. Children can make cool pools of water or other images a weary traveler might see on a hot desert day.
5. Help children attach the clear cellophane sheets (with the oasis designs) to the tops of their construction paper desert pictures using hinges of tape. When a cellophane oasis is lifted, it will reveal the true picture beneath.
6. Post the pictures on a "Marvelous Mirages" bulletin board.

Fun Fact:
The proof that mirages do exist—and are not figments of the imagination—is that mirages can be photographed.

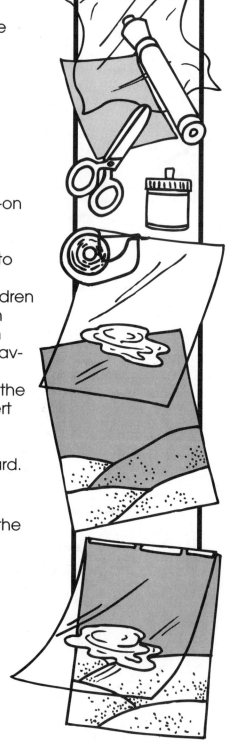

Funny Forecasts

Materials:
"Mother Goose Weather" Hands-on Handout (p. 20), crayons or markers, drawing paper

Directions:
1. Duplicate a copy of the "Mother Goose Weather" Hands-on Handout for each child.
2. Have children keep the handouts to refer to when the types of weather that are mentioned occur. Or post the handout in the classroom.
3. Have children keep track of how often these weather forecasts are correct. They can make check marks by the forecasts that are true and leave the others blank.
4. Be sure to mark important days on the calendar to observe: St. Swithin's Day (July 15th), Candlemas (February 2—same as Groundhog Day). Children can watch for the 40 days after St. Swithin's Day to see if the predictions are correct.
5. Let children illustrate Mother Goose's predictions for a Classroom Funny Forecasts book.

Option:
Once the children have observed some of the funny forecasts, continue in Mother Goose's footsteps and make a Creative Classroom Prediction book. Children can observe the weather, make their own predictions, and see if the predictions come true.

When clouds appear like rocks and towers,
The Earth's refreshed by frequent showers.

When the dew is on the grass,
Rain will never come to pass.

Rain on Sunday,
Sunshine on Monday.

A sunshiny shower
Won't last half an hour.

Mother Goose Weather

When clouds appear like rocks and towers,
The Earth's refreshed by frequent showers.

When the dew is on the grass,
Rain will never come to pass.

Rain before seven,
Fine before eleven.

St. Swithin's Day if thou dost rain,
For forty days it will remain.
St. Swithin's Day if thou be fair,
For forty days 'twill rain no more.

No weather is ill,
If the wind be still.

The south wind brings wet weather,
The north wind wet and cold together;
The west wind always brings us rain,
The east wind blows it back again.

If Candlemas Day be fair and bright,
Winter will have another flight;
If on Candlemas Day it be shower and rain,
Winter is gone, and will not come again.

Rain on Monday,
Sunshine next Sunday.

A sunshiny shower
Won't last half an hour.

Wacky Weather! © 1998 Monday Morning Books, Inc.

Jack Frost Fun

On a cold winter morning, have children look for frost on blades of grass, windowpanes, and leaves, or around keyholes.

Materials:
Large sheets of clear plastic or cellophane, black construction paper, scissors, glue in squeeze bottles, glitter or salt

Directions:
1. Ask if any of the children have ever seen dew on blades of grass in the morning. Then explain that frost forms instead of dew if the temperature is below freezing.
2. Divide each sheet of plastic into four sections using strips of black construction paper. This should look like a window with four panes.
3. Divide children into teams of four. Have each child decorate one "pane" using glue in squeeze bottles. While the glue is still wet, children should sprinkle glitter or salt over their designs and then shake off the excess.
4. The resulting frost pictures can be posted on windows so the light will shine through.

Fun Fact:
Hoar frost often forms around keyholes and delicate fern frost forms on windows.

Wacky Weather! © 1998 Monday Morning Books, Inc.

Terrible Tornado Game

Materials:
"Weather Playing Cards" (pp. 23-25), crayons or markers, scissors

Directions:
1. Make two copies of the "Weather Playing Cards," color, and cut apart. (Discard the second Tornado card.)
2. Laminate the playing cards and cut out again, leaving a thin, laminate border to prevent peeling.
3. Teach children how to play the game. The object is to collect the most pairs without getting caught with the Tornado card. (Children play the game like "Old Maid.")

How to Play the Game (2 to 4 players):
• Shuffle the cards and deal them, one at a time, face down to all players. Players may have extra cards.
• Players pick up their cards and see if there are any pairs. All matched pairs should be placed on the table, face up.
• One child is chosen to start. This child picks one card from the next player's hand (the player on the right).
• If the card drawn matches one in the first player's hand, the matched pair is placed face up on the table and the player picks again.
• If the card does not match, the new card is added to the player's hand and the next player takes a turn, choosing a card from the player on his or her right.
• The game continues until all pairs of cards are matched. The player with the most pairs is the winner. The player holding the Tornado card is the loser.

Notes:
• Remind children to hold their hands so that the other players cannot see which cards they are picking.
• As the children make sets, they set them down. The child who has the most sets is the winner.

Option:
For younger children, make two copies of each card and let the children play Concentration.

	☀	⛅	☁	🌧	🌨
31					
30					
29					
28					
27					
26					
25					
24					
23					
22					
21					
20					
19					
18					
17					
16					
15					
14					
13					
12					
11					
10					
9					
8					
7					
6					
5					
4					
3					
2					
1					

Weather Glossaries

Materials:
"Weather Glossary" Hands-on Handouts (pp. 29-30), writing paper, pens or pencils, dictionaries, construction paper, stapler, glue, scissors

Directions:
1. Duplicate the glossary pages, making one sheet for each child. Explain that a glossary is a list of words with definitions.
2. Have children look up each word in the dictionary.
3. Children should write the definition next to the word to create their own weather glossaries. (Younger children can draw pictures.)
4. As children learn new weather words, have them add the words to their weather glossaries.
5. Provide construction paper and a stapler for children to use to bind their pages together. They can decorate the covers with pictures of different types of weather.

Option:
White-out the words in the clouds and duplicate one page for each child. Have children write in their own weather-related words and definitions.

Wacky Weather! © 1998 Monday Morning Books, Inc.

Seasonal Spelling

Materials:
"Raindrop Patterns" (pp. 32-33), "Cloud Pattern" (p. 34), scissors, crayons or markers, tape or glue

Directions:
1. Duplicate the "Raindrop Patterns," making one sheet of each for each child and a few extra sheets for adult use.
2. Enlarge and duplicate the "Cloud Pattern," color, and post on the bulletin board. Cut out one extra set of "raindrops" and post them below the "Cloud Pattern."
3. Have children learn how to spell each word. They can pair off and test each other as a way of practicing.
4. Host a "Weather Spelling" contest in your classroom. Keep one set of "raindrops" in a hat and pull out one at a time, asking each child in turn to spell the word on the raindrop.
5. By process of elimination, continue with the spelling contest. (Children who misspell a word sit down. The rest continue to try to spell the words.)

Note:
For additional spelling words, refer to the "Weather A to Z List" (p. 77).

Options:
• Duplicate blank spelling raindrops, and let children write in their own weather-related words.
• Duplicate both the "Cloud Pattern" and the raindrops for younger children. They can simply glue or tape the raindrops to the cloud and practice tracing the words.

Raindrop Patterns

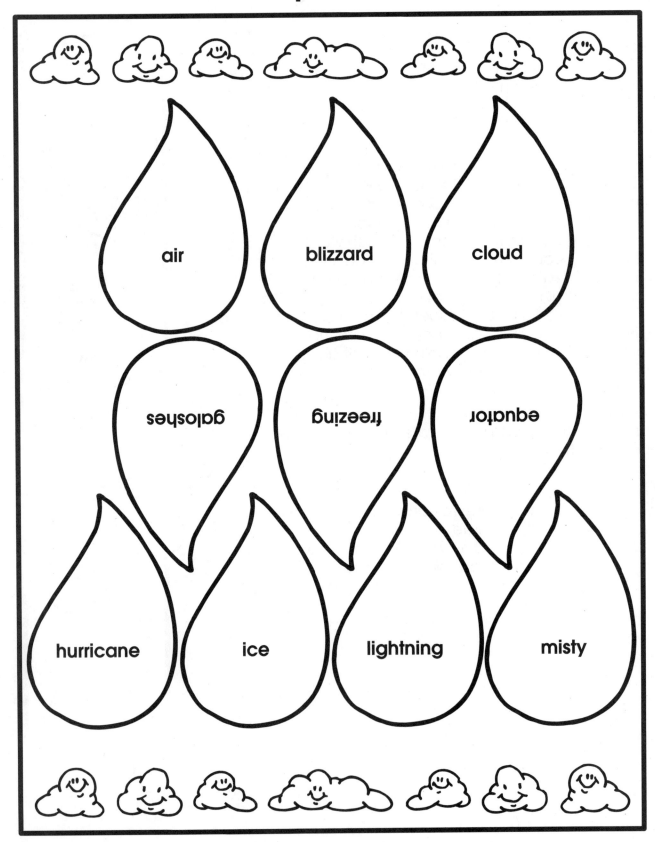

Raindrop Patterns

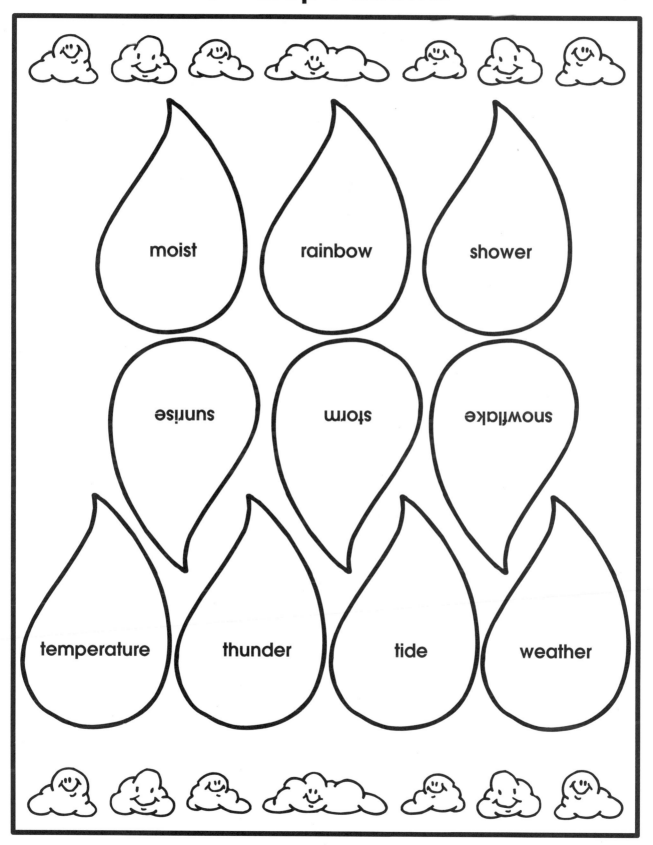

moist

rainbow

shower

sunrise

storm

snowflake

temperature

thunder

tide

weather

Cloud Pattern

Interview a Cloud

Materials:
"All About Clouds" Hands-on Handout (p. 18), "Cloud Fact Sheet" Hands-on Handout (p. 36), "Cloud Interview Sheet" Hands-on Handout (p. 37), pencils or markers

Directions:
1. In these reports, children research clouds and then play the part of their chosen clouds for an interview.
2. Duplicate one copy of the "All About Clouds" Hands-on Handout, the "Cloud Fact Sheet" Hands-on Handout, and the "Cloud Interview Sheet" Hands-on Handout for each child.
3. Let each child choose a cloud from the ones listed on page 18. Children can use the information on the sheet to research their clouds. Or they can use books from the library.
4. Have the children research their chosen clouds using the guidelines on the "Cloud Fact Sheet." Then have them write questions based on the facts using the "Cloud Interview Sheet."
5. Once the children have finished their research, divide them into pairs. Have each partner take a turn interviewing the other in front of the class.
6. Set up an interview schedule, perhaps working through five to six interviews per day.

Note:
Children can write reports on other weather-related topics (see the "Weather A to Z List," p. 77).

Options:
• Interviewers can hold microphones (cardboard tubes with egg carton sections glued to the top).
• Interviewees can also make simple costumes or masks to wear when they give their interviews.

Other Clouds:
• Altostratus
• Cirrocumulus
• Cirrostratus

Wacky Weather! © 1998 Monday Morning Books, Inc.

Cloud Fact Sheet

Use this fact sheet to record at least four facts about your chosen cloud. Remember to list the books you use. You can use the back of this sheet if you need more room.

My name is:
_____

My cloud is:
_____

Fact: _____

Fact: _____

Fact: _____

Fact: _____

Books I used:
_____

Title: _____

Author: _____

Title: _____

Author: _____

Cloud Interview Sheet

Write your answers under the questions. Write your own question for question 5. Your partner will use these questions to interview you in front of the class.

Question 1: What type of cloud are you?

_____

_____

Question 2: How high are you in the sky?

_____

_____

Question 3: What do you look like? (A large blanket? Feathers? Are you white, gray, or dark?)

_____

_____

Question 4: What type of weather do you like? (Calm? Clear? Cold?)

_____

_____

Question 5:

_____

_____

_____

Wacky Weather! © 1998 Monday Morning Books, Inc.

Lightning Reports

Very few people are struck by lightning. Tall trees and buildings are most at risk of being hit. Warn children not to stand near a tree in a storm. It is safest to be in a car, as the lightning will go into the ground through the rubber tires. Teach children the "Lightning Bolts" song (p. 63).

Materials:
"Types of Lightning" Hands-on Handout (p. 39), "Super-Duper Fact Card" on thunderstorms (p. 75), yellow and gray construction paper, scissors, pens or pencils, hangers, hole punch, yellow or gray yarn (or clear wire), tape or glue

Directions:
1. Duplicate a copy of the "Types of Lightning" Hands-on Handout for each child.
2. Have each child make a lightning bolt from yellow construction paper. They can make zigzag shapes or make any of the shapes described on the handout.
3. Have each child choose one or two facts to write on the lightning bolts.
4. Show children how to punch a hole in the top of each lightning bolt.
5. Divide children into teams of four or five. Have each team cover a hanger with gray construction paper to look like a thundercloud (cumulonimbus cloud).
6. Help children attach their lightning bolts to the bottoms of the hangers.
7. Hang the thundercloud reports in the classroom or in the library. Make sure to hang the clouds low enough for people to read the facts on the lightning bolts.

Fun Fact:
If you hear a thunderclap five seconds after you see a flash, the storm is about 1.2 miles (2 km.) away.

Types of Lightning

• Forked lightning has many branches.

• Pearl necklace lightning has points of extra brightness.

• Ribbon lightning follows a bent path.

• Rocket lightning travels slowly.

• Sheet lightning flashes behind a cloud.

• Streak lightning has one main stroke and many smaller shoots.

• Fireballs are glowing balls of lightning about the size of a beach ball. They zigzag from place to place. This is a rare form of lightning.

• Lightning always takes the quickest path to the ground.

• Lightning and thunder occur at the same time. You see lightning first because light travels faster than sound.

Wacky Weather! © 1998 Monday Morning Books, Inc.

Animal Weather Report

Superstitions are beliefs held in spite of evidence to the contrary. Often the beliefs are results of faith in chance. Many of the predictions listed on the following page are based on superstitions, but some are true.

Materials:
"Animal Knowledge" Hands-on Handout (p. 41), "Animal Weather Report" Hands-on Handout (p. 42), scissors, pens or pencils, crayons or markers

Directions:
1. Duplicate a copy of both handouts for each child. Fold the "Animal Knowledge" handouts in half and have children look only at the superstitions.
2. Discuss superstitions with the children.
3. Go over the superstitions on the handout. Children can vote on the ones they think are useable weather indicators and the ones that are solely superstitions. Check the answers.
4. Have each child choose an animal listed on the "Animal Knowledge" handout to research. The children can answer the questions on the "Animal Weather Report" handout using the "Animal Knowledge" handout. Or they can check out books or Web sites on animals as weather predictors. (See Nonfiction Resources.)
5. At the end of the "Animal Weather Reports," children write their own animal weather predictions, for example, "When cats sleep a lot, it's going to be hot." The predictions can be made up, or based on animal behavior they've observed.

Options:
• Children can report on other animals that are supposed to have weather prediction skills, including: owls, ants, crows, sea gulls, and seals (see chart in margin). Have children research the animals to find out the superstitions and the truth about the predictions.
• Bring a cricket into the classroom to test the temperature.
   Cricket's chirps in 15 seconds + 37 = degrees F
   Cricket's chirps in 8 seconds + 4 = degrees C
These formulas will give the correct temperature within one degree with 90% accuracy.

• **Seals:** When seals disappear through holes in the ice, a herbie (mini-blizzard) is about to hit. (True.)
• **Owls:** The hooting of an owl, means weather will be foul. (A good weather indicator because birds feel small changes in the air.)
• **Sea gulls:** Sitting gulls are a sign of rain. (True. Before a storm, the air is less able to support birds. It's harder to fly, so gulls are more likely to sit.)
• **Crows:** Expect it to be fair when crows fly in pairs. (A true indicator of good weather, since crows feed in groups but seek shelter separately.)
• **Ants:** When ants travel in a line, expect rain. When they scatter, expect fair weather. (Have children check for themselves.)

Animal Knowledge

SUPERSTITION

• If a groundhog pops out of its hole on February 2 and sees its shadow it means six more weeks of winter.

• When sheep huddle, tomorrow brings puddles.

• When ladybugs swarm, expect a day that's warm.

• When crickets slow their ticks, when pigs carry sticks, when ladybugs try to swarm, the animals together foretell the weather.

• When a beaver carries sticks in its mouth, it'll be a hard winter—you'd better go south.

TRUTH

• Punxsutawney Phil, a famous groundhog, is wrong about the weather more often than right.

• Sheep huddling to keep warm can mean rain is near.

• Ladybugs fly to cool down. This may be a sign of hot weather.

• Animals and insects are more sensitive to small weather changes than humans are. Their behavior can mean that weather is about to change.

• Native Indians thought this was a sign beavers were building stronger homes, but this isn't a reliable sign of harsh weather.

Animal Weather Report

My name is:

_____

My animal is:

_____

1. How does your animal foretell the weather?

_____

_____

2. What type of weather does your animal forecast?

_____

_____

3. Is your animal usually right or wrong?

_____

4. Draw a picture of your animal in the box below:

[   ]

5. My own animal weather prediction is:

_____

_____

Wacky Weather! © 1998 Monday Morning Books, Inc.

Amazing Auroras

Materials:

"Super-Duper Fact Card" on auroras (p. 69), colored tissue paper, liquid laundry starch, paintbrushes, tracing paper or clear cellophane or clear plastic sheets (the kind used to make transparencies), colored construction paper, tape or glue, markers, scissors

Directions:

1. Give each child a sheet of tracing paper or clear cellophane or plastic.
2. Children will tear colored tissue paper into strips and attach the strips to the background sheets. They can paint the tracing paper or cellophane with starch and then stick the tissue to it. Or they can place the strips of tissue in their desired pattern and coat the tissue with the starch. Overlapping the tissue paper creates interesting effects.
3. While the aurora pictures dry, have children research auroras. They can use the information on the "Super-Duper Fact Card" on auroras or choose facts from books, such as the ones listed below.
4. Make a construction paper border for each child's aurora by folding a sheet of construction paper in half and cutting out a rectangle in the center. The remaining paper will be a frame.
5. Have children write one or two aurora facts on their construction paper frames.
6. Help children attach the frames to the aurora pictures using tape or glue.
7. Post the auroras in a window, where the light can shine through the colored tissue.

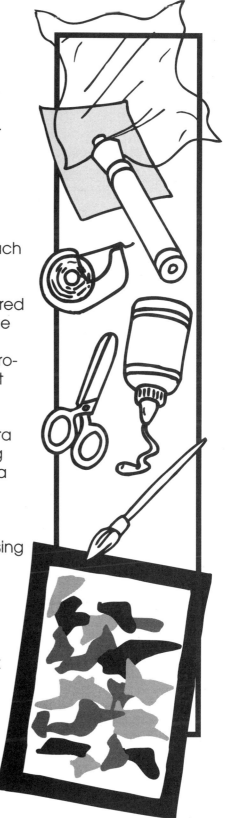

Aurora Books:

• *Aurora: The Mysterious Northern Lights* by Candace Sherk Savage (Sierra Club Books, 1994).
• *The Aurora Watchers Handbook* by Neil T. Davis (University of Alaska Press, 1992).
• *Northern Lights* by Dorothy M. Souza (Carolrhoda Books, 1994).

Interplanetary Weather

Materials:
"Planetary Weather" Hands-on Handouts (pp. 45-46),
"The Weather Report" Hands-on Handout (p. 47)

Directions:
1. Duplicate a copy of the "Planetary Weather" and "The Weather Report" Hands-on Handouts for each child.
2. Have children choose planets to research.
3. Children can use the information on the "Planetary Weather" handouts to answer questions on "The Weather Report" handout. They can do additional research about planets using the books listed in Nonfiction Resources.
4. Give each child a chance to report on the weather. Set up a table in front of the classroom. Children can pretend to be weather reporters on other planets, giving the other Martians, Venusians, Plutonians, etc., their daily weather.

Options:
• Let children dress in costume to give the weather on the distant planets. Simple costumes can be made from paper grocery bags and tempera paint. Masks can be made from paper plates.
• Have children watch the weather report on the news to get an idea of how weather forecasters act. Or, bring in a video tape of several weather forecasters (male and female) from different stations.
• Videotape children giving their reports.

There will be snow on Mars today with possible hail.

Wacky Weather! © 1998 Monday Morning Books, Inc.

Planetary Weather

Average daytime temperature on the planets:

Mercury	410 degrees C	770 degrees F
Venus	447 C	837 F
Earth	14 C	57 F
Mars	-125 C to 30 C	-193 F to 86 F
Jupiter	-140 C to 24 C	-220 F to 75 F
Saturn	-180 C	-292 F
Uranus	-216 C	-357 F
Neptune	-220 C	-364 F
Pluto	-230 C	-382 F

Mercury Facts:
• Mercury is almost airless.
• Mercury is very hot during the day.
• Mercury is very cold at night.
• Day and night last a long time on Mercury.

Venus Facts:
• On Venus, it is so hot that you'd vaporize if you weren't wearing special protective gear.
• On Venus, the sun rises in the west.
• Venus is always hidden behind thick, white clouds.
• There is little water on the planet. The clouds are made of droplets of acid.
• There are fast winds on the planet.

Mars Facts:
• Cold winds create frosty, dirty dust storms.
• The weather varies widely. At midday, you could go barefoot, but have to wear a wool hat.
• Sudden temperature changes may be caused by wind gusts that stir up warmer air from the ground.
• During the day, the clouds burn off and the skies turn a solid pink.

Wacky Weather! © 1998 Monday Morning Books, Inc.

Planetary Weather

Jupiter Facts:
• Thick clouds cover Jupiter.
• The clouds are red, orange, tan, and yellow.
• Jupiter's clouds are made of gas.
• The temperature is cold at the top layer of clouds and warmer at the bottom.

Saturn Facts:
• Saturn is circled by bands of clouds.
• The clouds are much paler than Jupiter's.
• Saturn is cold because it is far away from the sun. It is colder than the coldest place on Earth.
• Saturn has storms and strong, swirling winds.
• The winds blow much faster than even the strongest winds on Earth.

Uranus Facts:
• Blue-green clouds blow across the surface.
• At the tops of the clouds, it is colder than the coldest spot on Earth.
• Past the clouds, the atmosphere is hotter.

Neptune Facts:
• Neptune has the most wind of all the planets.
• Giant, dark hurricanes rage on Neptune.
• White methane ice clouds cover the surface.
• A huge tropical storm is always blowing on Neptune.

Pluto Facts:
• Pluto is very cold.
• It hardly gets any heat or light from the sun.
• During winter, the gases in its atmosphere freeze and it gets a coat of methane snow.
• In summer, the frozen methane turns to gas.

The Weather Report

My name is:

_____

I am reporting on the planet:

_____

The average daily temperature on my planet is:

_____

You need the following types of clothing to visit my planet:

_____

_____

The weather on my planet is (write brief description): _____

_____

_____

My planet looks like this: (Draw a picture below or on the back of the page.)

Wacky Weather! © 1998 Monday Morning Books, Inc.

The Wizard of Oz

Story:

The Wizard of Oz by L. Frank Baum (Doubleday, 1950). Dorothy lives in Kansas with her uncle and aunt. When a tornado hits, Dorothy and her dog Toto are whisked away in their house to a faraway country of amazing beauty. It is an entirely different world from the gray prairies Dorothy is used to. In this land, called Oz, Dorothy has a magnificent adventure, but finally she is able to return home to Kansas and to her family.

Setting the Stage:

• Build a scarecrow with the children and post it in one corner of the classroom.
• Learn about tornados. Refer to the "Super-Duper Fact Card" (p. 76).
• Show the movie *The Wizard of Oz*, and have children compare and contrast differences between the film and the book.

Tricky Tongue Twister:

• *A blustery blizzard baffled the wizard.*

The Blizzard of Oz

In *The Wizard of Oz*, a tornado blows Dorothy to Oz. In this activity, the children imagine that the title of the book has changed to a weather form. Then they draw book covers for the new Oz books.

Materials:
Drawing paper, crayons or markers

Directions:
1. Explain that children will be drawing book covers for stories. In the stories, the children will have been transported from their hometown to Oz.
2. Have children choose a type of wacky weather that might blow, whirl, snow, rain, or twirl them to another land. Children can choose a weather form from the list below, or from others they've studied, or they might choose a tornado, like the one in *The Wizard of Oz*.
3. Have children use art materials to make book covers for their imaginary stories, for example, the *Mirage of Oz* or the *Sandstorm of Oz*.
4. Post the completed stories and pictures on a "Blizzard of Oz" bulletin board.

Types of Weird Weather:
• A herbie is a wall of snow that hits suddenly. One minute the sun is shining, the next a mini-blizzard hits.
• A chinook is a hot, dry wind that can turn winter into summer in only a few minutes.
• Hurricanes are severe tropical storms that appear in the Atlantic.
• Typhoons are severe tropical storms in the western Pacific and China Sea.

Option:
Have children create short stories to go with their book covers in which a weird weather type brings them to an imaginary land.

Wacky Weather! © 1998 Monday Morning Books, Inc.

The Story of a Boy...

Story:

The Story of a Boy Named Will, Who Went Sledding Down the Hill by Daniil Kharms (North-South, 1993).
In this rhyming tale, Will picks up more and more creatures on his sled as he maneuvers down the hillside. The clever rhyme and snowy pictures enhance this story's appeal.

Setting the Stage:

• Decorate the windows with white doilies or snowflake patterns cut from white paper.
• Read other snow-themed books, such as *The Snowman* by Raymond Briggs or a version of *The Mitten*.
• Provide cotton balls for children to glue together to make snowmen. Children can add features with colored markers or bits of felt.
• Let children make snowpeople from marshmallows and toothpicks. Bits of black licorice can be attached for the features.
• Discuss where snow comes from. Refer to the "Super-Duper Fact Card" (p. 75).

Tricky Tongue Twister:

• *Nobody knows where melting snow goes.*

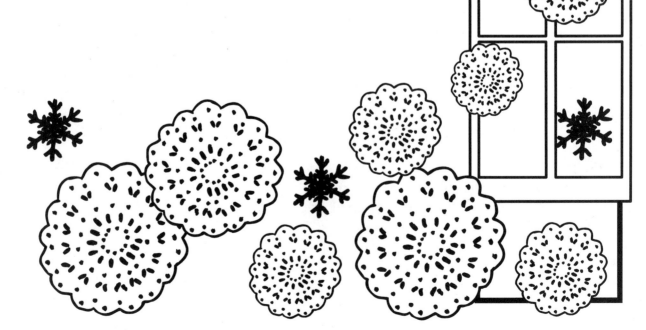

Rhymes with "Snow"

Materials:
Lined paper, pencils or pens

Directions:
1. After reading *The Story of a Boy Named Will*, give your children their own chance to make up rhyming weather tales.
2. Discuss the fact that in the story there are a few repetitive rhymes. Children can create similarly styled stories, or they can try to rhyme every line.
3. Begin with simple rhymes. Write several weather-related words on the board and have children brainstorm rhymes. Or use the suggested rhyming words below:

snow:	know	go	flow	mow
rain:	cane	pane	lane	main
hail:	rail	mail	pail	sail
cloud	crowd	loud	plowed	
wind:	grinned	pinned		

4. Have children string several words together to make a rhyme. They can start by putting their own names in the rhyme from *The Story of a Boy Named Will*, for example:

Anna went for a sled ride
And slid swiftly down the hillside.
Down the hill she slid her sled,
And hit a hunter as she sped.

Then they can change the words to make the rhyme their own:

Anna went for a ride in the snow.
She went as quickly as the sled would go.
Down the hill, beneath the clouds,
She slid her sled before a crowd.

5. Have children make covers for their own snow-related stories. Or they can write and illustrate their own books.

Wacky Weather! © 1998 Monday Morning Books, Inc.

The Stranger

Story

The Stranger by Chris Van Allsburg (Houghton Mifflin, 1986). A stranger is hit by a farmer's car and loses his memory. The family takes him in and cares for him, but the stranger does not remember who he is or what his job is. Even stranger, the weather around the farmhouse remains warm and sunny even though the calendar shows that autumn should be starting. Who is the stranger and what can't he remember?

Setting the Stage:

• This book is the perfect introduction into a unit on seasons. Whatever time of year you read this book, post seasonal icons on a bulletin board: red and yellow leaves for autumn, snowflakes cut from paper for winter, buds and young flowers for spring, and a bright yellow paper sun for summer.
• Discuss what happens to leaves to make them change. Refer to nonfiction resources, such as *How Leaves Change* by Sylvia A. Johnson (Lerner, 1986).
• Adopt a deciduous tree (a tree with leaves that change) in your school yard or nearby. Have children draw pictures of it throughout the year.
• Make notes of the weather on the first day of each season.

Tricky Tongue Twister:

• *Autumn's breezy, winter's sneezy, spring is easy, summer's fun.*

Summer All the Time

Materials:
Writing paper, pens or pencils

Directions:
1. Have children imagine that the stranger never remembers his job. Now, it is summer all the time.
2. Have children write down what would happen if the seasons never changed—if it never were autumn, winter, or spring. What would they miss? What would they be happy about?
3. Then have children imagine that they are able to change the weather like the stranger in the book *The Stranger*.
4. Ask the children to brainstorm what they would do: would they make it summer during winter vacation? Would snow days take up most of the year?
5. Have children write short paragraphs about what they would do if they could change the weather.
6. Provide crayons or markers for children to use to illustrate their stories.

Option:
On a winter day, have children draw pictures of summer fun: beaches, sand castles, sunny days, and so on. Post the pictures all around the room and have children pretend that it is a warm summer day. Do the reverse on a too-hot day: have children draw wintertime pictures and pretend it's cold out!

Water Dance

Story:
Water Dance by Thomas Locker (Harcourt, 1997).
In this beautifully illustrated book, different forms of water are
described in the first person: a cloud, a storm front, a thunder-
head, and so on. Scientific explanations about the different
forms of water can be found at the back of the book.

Setting the Stage:
• Provide a variety of nonfiction weather photo books for
children to look at. (See Nonfiction Resources.)
• Have children write their own weather descriptions in the
first person, for example, "I am a thunderstorm" or "I am a
hurricane," with descriptions that follow. Post these with illustrations around the classroom or bind in a classroom book.
• Discuss the concept of giving people's names to hurricanes.
Have children name other weather forms, such as sunny days,
thunderstorms, hail, and so on.

Tricky Tongue Twister:
• *Showers bring flowers, but sun brings fun.*

I Am...

Materials:
Index cards (one per child), pens or pencils, tape, student photos (optional)

Directions:
1. After reading *Water Dance*, have children practice describing themselves using colorful words. They should describe their personalities, likes and dislikes, and favorite activities, as well as physical appearance. (For example: "I am a writer, a light-footed dancer, a cheerful ice cream eater....") They can do this in the same format as in *Water Dance*, listing their descriptions and ending with the words "I am X." (Their names go in the blank.)
2. Have children write their descriptions on the lined sides of the index cards.
3. On the back of the cards, either write the children's names, or post their photos. Post the photos or write the names up-side-down, so that when the cards are lifted the pictures or names are right-side up.
4. Use a hinge of tape to fasten each index card on a bulletin board. Make sure that the descriptions are face front.
5. Invite the children to read each description and guess who wrote it before lifting the card to see either the picture or the person's name.

Option:
Have children use weather words to describe themselves, for example, "When I am angry, I am like a thunderstorm. When I am happy, my smile is as bright as a rainbow."

Wacky Weather! © 1998 Monday Morning Books, Inc.

The Snow Queen

Story:
The Snow Queen by Hans Christian Andersen.
After a bit of a broken, evil mirror gets into a little boy's eyes, the little boy is mesmerized and captured by the hauntingly beautiful Snow Queen. Meanwhile, a little girl tries to rescue him. After a long adventure, the girl finally arrives at the Snow Queen's palace, where the northern lights blaze strong and bright. The girl rescues the boy and her love melts the queen's spell and frees him.

Setting the Stage:
• Post mirrors around the room.
• Have children draw self-portraits based on their reflections.
• Help children locate the North Pole on the globe.
• Show pictures of the northern lights (aurora borealis) and southern lights (aurora australis) in nonfiction books (see Nonfiction Resources).
• Have children draw their own aurora pictures using colored chalk on dark construction paper backgrounds.

Other Snow Queen Versions:
• *Michael Hague's Favourite Hans Christian Andersen Fairy Tales* by Hans Christian Andersen (Holt, 1981).
This book includes nine Andersen tales.
• *The Snow Queen* adapted by Amy Ehrlich, illustrated by Susan Jeffers (Dial, 1982).
Beautiful illustrations make this book worthwhile, despite long text.
• *The Snow Queen* translated by Naomi Lewis, illustrated by Angela Barrett (Holt, 1988).
• *Snow Queen* (CBS/Fox Video, 1983).
This Faerie Tale Theatre production features Melissa Gilbert, Lee Remick, Lauren Hutton, and others.

Tricky Tongue Twister:
• *Don't slight the sights of the northern lights.*

The Sun Queen

In this activity, children create a palace suitable for the character who is the oposite of the Snow Queen.

Materials:
Cardboard box and round oatmeal boxes, yellow or gold construction paper, glue, scissors, decorative items (buttons, ribbons, lace)

Directions:
1. Have children imagine that instead of the Snow Queen, the title character in this story is called the Sun Queen.
2. As a class, brainstorm differences that might occur in the story. For example, instead of bringing the little boy to an ice palace, the Sun Queen might take him to Hawaii.
3. Write down the descriptions of the Sun Queen.
4. Working together, let children create the Sun Queen's palace. Rather than being made of snow and ice, it might be made of golden sand and autumn leaves. Children can attach the oatmeal boxes to the main box to serve as towers.
5. Post the Sun Queen descriptions on a bulletin board near the palace.

Options:
• Show children pictures of other palaces, for example, the Taj Mahal or Versailles (the palace of the Sun King).
• In *The Snow Queen*, white-coated animals lived in the queen's palace. Have children research types of animals that live in hot climates. They can draw pictures of these animals and post them in their Sun Palace.

Wacky Weather! © 1998 Monday Morning Books, Inc.

Writing a Retold Tale

Often, authors use old stories as idea starters, changing specific details to make the stories their own. Share retold tales (listed below) with your students before doing this activity.

Materials:

"Writing a Retold Tale" Hands-on Handout (p. 59), writing paper, drawing paper, crayons or markers, pens or pencils, glitter and glue (optional)

Directions:

1. Explain that the children will be creating new versions of famous tales. In order to change their tales, they will create characters drawn from different types of weather. For example, a character might be a tornado queen, a thunderstorm king, and so on.
2. Choose an example of a tale to study with the children as a class. For example, in *The Snow Queen*, the coldly beautiful queen is able to freeze the little boy's heart and make him her captive. Have the children recall different ways the author described the Snow Queen. (They can refer to the story.)
3. Duplicate a copy of the "Writing a Retold Tale" Hands-on Handout for each child.
4. Provide crayons and drawing paper for children to use to draw pictures of their characters. Children can add glitter for extra sparkle.
5. Post the write-ups and the drawings together on a "Weather Royalty" bulletin board.

Option:

Children can write longer stories to be bound into a classroom book.

Retold Tales:

• *The Frog Prince Continued* by Jon Scieszka, paintings by Steve Johnson (Viking, 1991).
• *Jim and the Beanstalk* by Raymond Briggs (Coward, McCann, 1970).
• *The True Story of the 3 Little Pigs by A. Wolf* as told to Jon Scieszka, illustrated by Lane Smith (Viking, 1989).

Writing a Retold Tale

What You Do:
1. Choose a type of weather to write about.
2. Name your character after the type of weather, for example, the Blizzard Queen.
3. Describe the way your character looks.
4. Think about things your character might be able to do based on its weather name:
• Can it make the wind blow?
• Can it cause tornados to whirl?
• Can it leave its name written in frost on windows?
• Does it wear a rainbow?
5. Write a short story about your weather character. You can retell the story of the Snow Queen. Or you can retell a different story, like the ones listed below.
6. Draw a picture of your character.

Other Famous Tales to Retell:
• "Sleeping Beauty"
• "Cinderella"
• "Snow White"
• "The Little Mermaid"
• "Pinocchio"
• "Hansel and Gretel"
• "Goldilocks and the Three Bears"

Wacky Weather! © 1998 Monday Morning Books, Inc.

Wacky Weather Program

Songs:
- "Snow Business"
- "Lightning Bolts"
- "Let's Go to the Equator"
- "Hurricane"
- "Tornados Start Out as Big Rainstorms"
- "Rainbows and Moonbows"

Featuring:

Snow Business . . .

(to the tune of "There's No Business Like Show Business")

There's no business like snow business,
Like no business I know.
It's so cold that everyone is sneezing.
Sometimes a sharp wind begins to blow.
Look and see the temperature is freezing,
And that is when the rain turns to snow!

There's no people like snow people,
Like no people I know.
You can make a snowman
When it's really cold.
He'll have eyes made from lumps of coal.
And until the sun shines down he won't get old.
It's snow business, I know.
Let's go play in the snow!

Snow Costume

What You Need:
Large paper grocery bag, doilies, white tempera paint, shallow tins (for paint), scissors, glue, salt

What You Do:
1. Cut arm slits in the sides of the bag and a circle for your head to fit through.
2. Use the doilies to print snowflake patterns onto the bag. Dip the doilies in the tins of white paint and then press the doilies to the paper bag. Or glue doilies all over the bag.
3. Before the bag dries, sprinkle salt on top of the paint to make it sparkly.
4. Once the bag is dry, slide it on, and you're ready to sing!

Wacky Weather! © 1998 Monday Morning Books, Inc.

Lightning Bolts

(to the tune of "Jingle Bells")

Lightning bolts, thunderclouds, electric energy.
The sky lights up with fire, don't hide under trees.
Ice and water droplets inside stormy clouds
Are pushed and pulled apart so hard
They make a sound that's loud!

Way up in the clouds,
Ice and water clash.
We see lightning strike,
Then hear thunder crash!

When the lightning strikes,
It can cause a fire,
So find an open space,
Away from trees and wires.

Lightning bolts, thunderclouds, electric energy.
The sky lights up with fire, don't hide under trees.
Ice and water droplets inside stormy clouds
Are pushed and pulled apart so hard
They make a sound that's loud!

Note: Give children tambourines or cymbals to use to make noise at the end of the song.

Wacky Weather! © 1998 Monday Morning Books, Inc.

Thundercloud Costume

What You Need:
Two large pieces of thin cardboard, hole punch, twine, gray tempera paint, paintbrushes, scissors, marker

What You Do:
1. Draw a cloud shape on one piece of the cardboard and cut it out.
2. Use the first cloud to trace a matching cloud on the second piece of cardboard, and cut it out.
3. Hold up one cloud in front of you. Have a friend use a marker to make dots showing where the middle part of your shoulders are.
4. Line up the clouds again and punch two holes in each cloud. The holes should line up.
5. Paint one cloud gray.
6. Once the paint has dried, thread a piece of twine through the holes and tie.
7. Slip the clouds over your head, with the gray side out. Now you are ready to sing!

Option:
Make a headband to wear with your costume. You can add gold or yellow zigzags for lightning bolts.

Let's Go to the Equator

(to the tune of "Take Me Out to the Ball Game")

Let's go to the equator.
Let's go out in the sun.
Put on sunglasses whenever you play.
Wear 15 SPF sunscreen all day.

The equator's right in the middle,
Look for it on your school globe.
It's a made-up line circling Earth
Between both the poles.

Note: Have children wear sunglasses and straw hats while they sing this song.

Hurricane

(to the tune of "Row, Row, Row Your Boat")

Great, big storms roar out
Of the ocean blue
Hurricane, hurricane, hurricane, hurricane,
That's what some call you.

Wacky Weather! © 1998 Monday Morning Books, Inc.

Tornados Start Out...

(to the tune of "My Bonnie Lies Over the Ocean")

Tornados start out as big rainstorms
With dark clouds and huge, heavy rains.
Then lightning comes faster and faster,
And thunder roars like a freight train, a train.

Don't go out, don't go out,
When a tornado hits, stay inside.
Don't go out, don't go out,
Find a place where you can hide.

Tornados are sometimes called twisters.
Their winds spin around and around.
They suck up loose clay, dust, and soil.
Each time they touch down on the ground,
          the ground.

(Chorus)

Tornados cause terrible damage.
They turn houses back into bricks.
With winds strong enough to bend bridges,
Buildings are broken to bits, to bits.

(Chorus)

Note: In the Northern Hemisphere, tornado winds usually rotate in a counterclockwise direction. In the Southern Hemisphere, they rotate in a clockwise direction.

Rainbows and Moonbows

(to the tune of "Frosty the Snowman")

Rainbows are made of
Water droplets and sunshine.
When the rain bends light,
Seven colors bright
Appear in a curving line.

(to chorus tune)
These colors are in sunlight,
But they're hidden from our eyes.
It takes the sunlight mixed with rain
To reveal the great surprise.

Moonbows are made of
Water droplets and moonbeams.
When the moon shines bright
On a rainy night,
That's when moonbows can be seen.

(to chorus tune)
These colors are in moonlight,
But they're hidden from our eyes.
It takes the moonlight mixed with rain
To reveal the great surprise.

Wacky Weather! © 1998 Monday Morning Books, Inc.

Rainbow Costume

Materials:

Tempera paint in rainbow colors, paintbrushes, shallow tins (for paint), butcher paper, masking tape, clothes in rainbow colors

Directions:

1. Spread the butcher paper on the floor. Tape the edges with masking tape to secure.
2. Have the children use paintbrushes to create a large rainbow mural. Remind the children of the mnemonic Roy. G. Biv. Help them to make sure the rainbow stripes are in the correct order.
3. Once the paint is dry, post the mural as the backdrop on the stage.
4. Have each child who is singing wear a rainbow color.
5. Mix up the groups so that the rainbow colors are not in order.
6. As the children sing "Rainbows and Moonbows," have them move forward into groups that are all one color. For example, the children wearing orange will group together and the children wearing blue will group together.
7. As the children sing the last verse, have them arrange themselves into rainbow order. You can help simplify this for the children by assigning each color a number from one to seven. Explain that the ones will move to the first part of the stage, the twos will move to the next part, and so on.

Note:

If it is difficult for children to find appropriately colored clothing, have each child bring in a white t-shirt. Dye the clothing in batches to make sure you have enough reds, yellows, oranges, and so on.

Weather A to Z List

A: Atmosphere, Autumn
B: Breezes
C: Clouds
D: Drizzle
E: El Niño
F: Floods, Fog, Fogbow
G: Glaciers
H: Hail, Hurricanes
I: Ice, Icicles
J: Jet Stream, Jupiter
K: Krakatoa
L: Lightning
M: Mars, Mercury, Mirage, Monsoon
N: Neptune
O: Ozone Layer
P: Pluto, Polar Front
R: Rain, Rainbows
S: Saturn, Snow, Spring, Summer
T: Thunder, Twisters, Typhoons
U: Uranus
V: Venus
W: Wind, Winter
X: Xlokk Wind
Z: Zodiacal Light

Wacky Weather! © 1998 Monday Morning Books, Inc.

Beaufort Wind Scale

Admiral Beaufort invented this wind speed scale in 1805. The scale was intended for use at sea, but has been adapted for use on land. (To convert to mph, multiply the kph by .6214.)

Force	Strength	Kph	Effect
0	Calm	0-1	Smoke rises vertically
1	Light Air	1-5	Smoke slowly drifts
2	Light Breeze	6-11	Leaves rustle
3	Gentle Breeze	12-19	Twigs move
4	Moderate Breeze	20-29	Small branches move
5	Fresh Breeze	30-39	Small trees move
6	Strong Breeze	40-50	Large branches sway
7	Near Gale	51-61	Whole trees sway
8	Gale	62-74	Twigs break off trees
9	Strong Gale	75-87	Branches blown apart
10	Storm	88-101	Trees uprooted
11	Violent Storm	102-117	Damage to buildings
12	Hurricane	119+	Devastation

All About El Niño

El Niño is a type of unusual weather. The name is Spanish for "The Child." Fishermen in Peru named it El Niño because it usually comes around Christmas. El Niño is caused by a rise in ocean temperatures. The temperatures can be as high as ten degrees more than normal.

El Niño can cause a number of different types of weather. In the United States, El Niño can cause flooding and heavy storms. In Asia and Africa, El Niño can cause drought. Winters that are usually very cold can become much warmer. The large storms and floods can lead to landslides.

Nonfiction Resources

• *Aurora: The Mysterious Northern Lights* by Candace Sherk Savage (Sierra Club Books, 1994).
• *The Aurora Watchers Handbook* by Neil T. Davis (University of Alaska Press, 1992).
• *Hurricanes* by Patricia Lauber (Scholastic, 1996).
• *It's Raining Cats and Dogs* by Franklyn M. Branley, illustrated by True Kelley (Houghton Mifflin, 1987).
This book includes interesting information about animals as weather predictors to share with the children.
• *A January Fog Will Freeze a Hog* and Other Weather Folklore compiled and edited by Hubert Davis, illustrated by John Wallner (Crown, 1977).
This book includes superstitions, as well as real information about animals as weather predictors to share with the children.
• *Northern Lights* by Dorothy M. Souza (Carolrhoda Books, 1994).
• *Pluto: A Double Planet?* by Isaac Asimov (Gareth Stevens, 1990).
• *Seasons* by Melvin Berger (Doubleday, 1990).
• *Snowflakes* by Joan Sugarman, illustrated by Jennifer Dewey (Little, Brown, 1985).
• *Tornado* by Christopher Lampton (Millbrook, 1991).
• *The Usborne Book* of Weather Facts by Anita Ganeri (Usborne, 1987).
• *Weather* by Seymour Simon (Morrow, 1993).
• *Weather and Its Work* by David Lambert and Ralphy Hardy (Orbis, 1994).
• *The Weather Sky* by Bruce McMillan (Farrar, 1991).
• *Weatherwatch* by Valerie Wyatt (Addison-Wesley, 1990).
This book includes information about animals as weather predictors to share with the children.

Planet books by Seymour Simon:
• *Jupiter* (Morrow, 1985).
• *Mars* (Morrow, 1987).
• *Saturn* (Morrow, 1985).
• *Uranus* (Morrow, 1987).
• *Neptune* (Morrow, 1991).
• *Mercury* (Morrow, 1992).

Wacky Weather! © 1998 Monday Morning Books, Inc.

Web Site Addresses

Cloud Web Sites:
This site includes information about hurricanes and tornados, and how clouds form.
• Cloud Catalog
http://covis.atmos.uiuc.edu/guide/clouds/html/oldhome.html

El Niño Web Sites:
• What Is an El Niño?
http://www.pmel.noaa.gov/toga-tao/el-nino-story.html

Groundhog Web Sites:
• Punxsutawney Phil's Story
http://www.groundhog.org/history.html

Hurricane Web Sites
• Hurricanes
http://covis1.atmos.uiuc.edu/guide/clouds/storms/html/hurricane.html

Planet Web Sites:
• Welcome to the Planets
http://pds.jpl.nasa.gov/planets/

Waterspout Web Sites
• Waterspout Photographs
http://atmos.es.mq.edu.au/AMOS/weatherwatch/wspout.htm

Weather Web Sites:
• Rocky Mountain West
http://www.rmwest.com/resource/weather.htm

• The best efforts have been made to find current Web sites. However, Web sites sometimes change. In addition to using these sites, also try keyword searches, such as specific types of weather.